Some Words

Selected by

Charles Ellingworth

ISBN: 978-1-326-49494-0

PublishNation
www.publishnation.co.uk

WORDS

I read a lot; even a train ticket will do if there's nothing else about. I have kissed a lot of frogs along the way but there are things that have made me laugh, caused a catch in my voice when reading them out to someone else - or made me ponder.

It would be a shame not to share the benefit of all that frog kissing. There is neither a theme nor an index. This is a personal selection.

What would you do, and what would you be, if you weren't afraid?

There was never a child so lovely but his mother was glad to get him asleep.

Ralph Waldo Emerson

There's only one thing worse than camping, and that's camping with other people.

William Skidelsky

Live by the sword, die by the sword. I just didn't know there'd be so many swords.

Nick Clegg

If you would know the value of money, go and try to borrow some.

Benjamin Franklin

Ever since the French Revolution, people throughout the world have gradually come to see both equality and individual freedom as fundamental values. Yet the two values contradict each other. Equality can be ensured only by curtailing the freedoms of those who are better off. Guaranteeing that every individual will be free to do as he wishes inevitably short-changes equality. The entire political history of the world since 1789 can be seen as a series of attempts to reconcile this contradiction......

Just as mediaeval culture did not manage to square chivalry with Christianity, so the modern world fails to square liberty with equality. But this is no defect. Such contradictions are an inseparable part of human culture. In fact, they are culture's engines, responsible for the creativity and dynamism of our species. Just as when two clashing musical notes played together force the piece of music forward, so discord in our thoughts, ideas and values compel us to think, re-evaluate and criticise. Consistency is the playground of dull minds.

If tensions, conflicts and irresolvable dilemmas are the spice of every culture, a human being who belongs to any particular culture must hold contradictory beliefs and be riven by incompatible values. It's such an essential feature of any culture that it even has a name: cognitive dissonance. Cognitive dissonance is often considered a failure of the human psyche. In fact, it is a vital asset. Had people been unable to hold contradictory beliefs and values, it would probably have been impossible to establish and maintain any human culture.

If, say, a Christian really wants to understand the Muslims who attend that mosque down the street, he shouldn't look for a pristine set of values that every Muslim holds dear. Rather, he should enquire into the Catch-22s of Muslim culture, those places where rules are at war and standards scuffle. It's at the very spot where the Muslims teeter between two imperatives that you'll understand them best.

Yuval Noah Harari. Sapiens

You can't call this shit 'The War on Drugs'; wars end.

From 'The Wire'

It's a terrible thing to look over your shoulder when you are trying to lead and find no one there.

Franklin Roosevelt

Dubai is what would happen if you gave a twelve year old a trillion dollars to redecorate his bedroom.

Dane Baptiste

Dubai is like an entire city designed by Donald Trump.

Alex Proud

Henry Kissinger famously (and he says apocryphally) asked 'Who do I call if I want to speak to Europe.' Catherine Ashton, EU's Foreign Affairs Representative quipped...

Yes, Europe does have a number. It is mine. When you dial it you hear a computer. Press one for Germany, two for France, three for Britain...

Evelyn Waugh wrote a great Oxford novel. This is from an essay on his alma mater.

All the misunderstanding of the value of university life seems to me to come from two extreme heresies. On the one hand of those who expect a University to be a kind of insurance company in to which is so much money is paid and from which so much, eventually, is extracted. They expect a BA degree to be a badge which will gain them instant preference over poorer competitors, and in nine cases out of ten they are disappointed.

On the other hand there are those who expect Oxford to be like an Oxford novel. A place of easy living, subtle conversation, and illuminating friendships. They expect it to be a kind of microcosm of 18th-century Whig society, combined with an infinitely sophisticated modernism. They, too, are disappointed.

The truth is that Oxford is simply a very beautiful city in which it is convenient to segregate a certain number of the young of the nation while they are growing up. It is absurd to pretend that a boy of eighteen, however sound he has been as a school prefect, is a fully grown man. Those who choose or obliged to begin regular, remunerative, responsible work at the moment they leave school, particularly if they have had a fairly carefully tended adolescence, often shows signs of a kind of arrested development.

It is just because Oxford keep some back from their careers that it is of most value.

It gives them another four years in which to grow up gradually. It puts them out of the way of the fellow citizens while they're making fools of themselves. They can learn to get drunk or not to get drunk; they can edit their own papers and air their opinions; they can learn how to give parties; they can find out, before they are too busy, what really amuses and excites them; and they can do all this in the town by themselves.

After that they can begin on the dreary and futile jobs that wait for most of them, with a great deal more chance of keeping a sense of humour and self-respect.

True intelligence very readily conceives of an intelligence superior to its own; and this is why truly intelligent men are modest.

Andre Gide

This is Clive James reflecting on Joseph Conrad's 'Victory' as part of his reading and rereading in the face of his impending death from leukaemia. "If you don't know the exact moment when the lights will go out, you might as well read until they do."

The first big slaughterhouse battles of the First World War had already been fought when Conrad was publishing the novel (Victory) but there is not a hint of pacifism. Conrad knew that unarmed goodwill is useless against armed malice. It was to be a lesson that the coming century would teach over and over, and so on into the present century: peace is not a principle, it is only a desirable state of affairs, and can't be obtained without a capacity for violence at least equal to the balance of the threat. Conrad didn't want to reach this conclusion any more than we do, but his artistic instincts were proof against the slightest tinge of mystical spiritual solace, and so should ours be. Our age of massacres has also been an age of the intellectual charlatan, when people claiming to interpret events can barely be relied upon to give a straightforward account of what actually happened. Conrad was the writer who reached political adulthood before any of the other writers of his time, and when they did, they reached only to his knee.

That being said, however, it must be admitted that Heyst's upright stupidity grows tedious in the final scenes. Conrad should have made his hero as intelligent as himself, the better to illustrate his thematic concern with how the historic forces that crush the naive will do the same to the wise, if they do not prepare to fight back. Finally, he tends to reinforce our wishful thought that cultivation – gained, for example, from reading a novel by Conrad – might be enough to ward of barbarism. But barbarism doesn't care if we are cultivated or not.

The same amount of money is spent on presents in Japan as Americans invest in justice. It so happens that that Japan is the developed country with the least expenditure for justice per person in the world.

Hector Garcia: A geek in Japan

I had read Keynes's insight into the nature of the banker...

The "sound" banker alas! is not the one who sees danger and avoids it, but one who, when he is ruined, is ruined in the conventional and orthodox way along with his fellows, so that no one can really blame him.

But I hadn't read the rest...

It is necessarily part of the business of a banker to maintain appearances and to profess a conventional respectability, which is more than human. Lifelong practices of this kind make them the most romantic and least realistic of men.

Freddie experienced the sort of abysmal soul-sadness which afflicts one of Tolstoy's Russian peasants when, after putting in a heavy day's work strangling his father, beating his wife and dropping the baby into the city's reservoir, turns to the cupboard to find the vodka bottle empty.

PG Woodhouse

There will always be a reason why you meet people. Either you need them to change your life or you're the one that will change theirs.

Angel Harifa

Since none of us know where we are going, it is important that we all stick together in case someone gets there.

Ken Kasey

Freedom of the press is limited to those that own one.

AJ Liebling

For forms of government let fools contest
What're is best administer'd is best

Alexander Pope

The Monetary Union will boil down to a giant extortion scheme. One day German taxpayers will say 'we have to bankroll the loafers who enjoy the easy life in cafes on southern beaches.' When we dare to call for more monetary discipline the profligate countries will claim that such containment is responsible for their financial difficulties, and they will blame us for it. This way we risk again becoming the most hated people in Europe.

Arnulf Baring, German political advisor in 1997

There are two ways to be fooled. One is to believe something that is not true; The other is not to believe something that is.

Kierkegaard

I've learned that your intuition about things you don't know much about isn't very good.

Larry Page

Two dyslexics sitting together.
'Can you smell smoke?'
'Can't even spell my own name'

Many of the political machinations of the early Roman republic could probably be dropped seamlessly onto the front page of today's Politico. These things never really change. It would be a mistake, however, to apply that same reasoning to the impact of advancing technology.

Up until the moment the first aircraft achieved sustained powered flight at Kitty Hawk, North Carolina, it was an incontrovertible fact — supported by data stretching back to the beginning of time —that human beings, strapped into heavier-than-air contraptions, do not fly. Just as that reality shifted in an instant, a similar phenomenon plays out continuously in nearly every sphere of technology. This time is always different where technology is concerned: that, after all, is the entire point of innovation.

Martin Ford, Rise of the Robots

My mother is far too intelligent to understand anything she doesn't like.

Arnold Bennett

In July 2014, the Special Inspector General for Afghanistan Reconstruction, in its quarterly report to Congress, found that "by the end of 2014, the US will have committed more funds to reconstruct Afghanistan, in inflation-adjusted terms, than it spent on 16 European countries after the Second World War under the Marshall Plan." Academic assessments also put the total cost to the US of the Afghan and Iraq wars at up to a third of the current $18 trillion national debt.

Charisma is the ability to influence without logic.

Quentin Crisp

The majority of people perform well in a crisis and when the spotlight is on them; it's on the Sunday afternoons of this life, when nobody is looking, that the spirit falters.

Alan Bennett

Give us this day our daily idea, and forgive us what we thought yesterday.

Bernard Berenson's daily prayer

Slumbering in every human being lies an infinity of possibilities, which one must not arouse in vain. For it is terrible when the whole man resonates with echoes and echoes, none becoming a real voice.

Elias Canetti: Notes from Hampstead

We use the word "guru" because "charlatan" is too long to fit into a headline.

Peter Drucker

Near the dogleg turn of the lane down to the ponies' field,
skulking in summer among cow parsley and meadow sweet,
in winter with their streaked black corrugated walls laid bare,
were the half-dozen Nissen huts my father refused to mention.
A prisoner of war camp for Italian soldiers, my mother told me,
but also part of the silence my father had bought back with him
ten years before from Germany which now could not be ended
although the reason for that was one more thing he never gave.
Why spoil and an early morning stroll bringing halters for the ponies
so we could lead them home to the stable yard then saddle up?
What else could there possibly be on earth for us to talk about
that was more interesting than a blackbird calling in the hedge,
or the swarming hawthorn flowers that smelled faintly of drains,
or the rain cloud that he always said was only a clearing shower.

Andrew Motion

Sometimes you get the best light from a burning bridge.

Don Henley

Live like you were going to die tomorrow, and learn as if you were
going to live forever.

Ghandi

Knowledge is like a sphere, the greater its volume, the larger its
contact with the unknown.

Pascal

If our brains were simple enough, we wouldn't be smart enough to
understand them.

What terrorist fundamentalist lack is a feature it is easy to discern in all authentic fundamentalists, from Tibetan Buddhists to the Amish: The absence of resentment and envy, the deep indifference to the nonbeliever's way of life. If today's so-called fundamentalists really believe that they have found their way to truth, why do they feel threatened by non-believers? When a Buddhist encounters a Western hedonist, he hardly condemns. He just benevolently notes that the hedonist's search for happiness is self-defeating. In contrast, the terrorist fundamentalists are deeply bothered, intrigued, fascinated by the sinful life of the non-believers. One can feel that, in fighting the sinful other, they are fighting their own temptations.

Slavoj Zizek

This is Gladstone's proposal letter to Catherine Glynne. It's amazing she had any idea what he was asking in what must be the most convoluted sentence in the English language. Romantic it is not. As Disraeli remarked 'He is a man overcome by the exuberance of 'his own verbosity.'

I seek much in a wife in gifts better than those of our human pride, and am also sensible that she can find little in me: sensible that, were you to treat this note as the offering of utter presumption, I must not be surprised: sensible that the lot I invite you to share, even it be not attended, as I trust it is not, with particular disadvantages of an outward kind, is one, I do not say unequal to your deserts, that were in saying little, but liable at best to changes and perplexities and pains which, for myself, I contemplate without apprehension, but to which it is perhaps selfishness in the main, with the sense of inward dependence counteracting an opposite sense of my too real unworthiness, which would make me contribute to expose another - and that other!

I won't insult your intelligence by suggesting that you really believe what you just said.

William F Buckley

Of all the icy blasts that blow on love, a request for money is the most chilling and havoc-wreaking

Flaubert

Lebanon has the highest proportion of refugees in any country on the globe. In Britain, it would be like the entire population of Norway, Nicaragua, Denmark and Croatia turning up penniless on the south coast.

The fear of death follows from the fear of life. A man who lives fully is prepared to die at any time.

Mark Twain

I've always regarded the French as being basically untrustworthy because they use the same word for 'straight on' as 'turn right'.

Jonathan Ruffer

The older I get, the older old is.

Tom Baker

All great states found themselves upon an outrage of nature, from which springs both their vigor and their vulnerability. Athens' derangement is democracy. To the good, this species of license unleashes enterprise in the citizenry unknown in more closely governed states, and these energies may propel the nation to unprecedented prosperity. Its mischief is the envy it loses in the body politic. Democracy devours its young. The higher a man ascends, the more fervidly do his fellows work to procure his downfall, so that when an individual of legitimate greatness does arise, the state may make use of him a moment only before the mob lashes his limbs to the stake and fires the brands at his feet.

Lysander, Sparta's great military leader

It came out of the future which didn't exist yet, into the present that had no duration, and went into the past which had ceased to exist. I don't know that we can understand time any better than a child.

St. Augustine, when asked where time came from.

It is unwise for two people to love each other before they know each other.

Emile Dard

Every man has his secret sorrows which the world knows not; and often times we call a man cold when he is only sad.

Henry Wadsworth Longfellow

Madam, Mr Disraeli has had to make his position, and men who make their position will say and do things which are not necessary to be said or done by those for whom positions have been provided.

Lord Derby to Queen Victoria 1851

Lawyers, I suppose, were children once.

Charles Lamb

You can stand firm in a fight against everything except kindness.

Jean Jacques Rousseau

Bad Blood by Lorna Sage is a memoir of post war rural Wales and her dysfunctional family. You can smell the genteel poverty and feel the itch of austerity. It also has a wonderful opening paragraph....

Grandfather's skirts would flap in the wind along the churchyard path and I would hang on. He often found things to do in the vestry, excuses for getting out of the vicarage (kicking the swollen door cursing) and so long as he took me he couldn't get up to much. I was a sort of hobble; he was my minder and I was his. He would have liked to have got further away but petrol was rationed. The church was it least safe. My grandmother never went near it, except feet first in her coffin, but that was years later, when she was buried in the same grave as him. Rotting together for eternity, one flesh at the last after a lifetime's mutual loathing. In life though, she never invaded his patch; once inside the churchyard gate he was on his own ground, in his element. He was good at funerals, being gaunt and lined, marked with mortality. He had a scar down his hollow cheek too, which Grandma had done with a carving knife one of the many times he came home pissed and incapable.

Jeremy Thorpe died recently, bringing back memories of his fall from grace in the 1970s. It was farce mixed with tragedy as Francis Wheen well tells it in reviewing Michael Bloch's biography.

Did Thorpe mean to kill Scott or merely to give him a fright. Either way it's a preposterous yarn, expertly narrated by Bloch in which the best man from Thorpe's wedding consults a Welsh carpet merchant, who recruits a Swansea nightclub owner, who hires an airline pilot and part time hit man named Andrew 'Gino Newton, who shoots Scott's Great Dane, Rinka – as a consequence of which Thorpe is accused of conspiracy to murder and the late editor of the Literary Review, Auberon Waugh, stands for Parliament against him on behalf of the Dog Lovers' Party.

At which point you may scratch your ear and think: can any of this be true? It reads like a shaggy-dog story, fittingly enough, and credulity is stretched even further by some of Bloch's supporting cast: DCS Proven Sharpe, head of Devon and Cornwall. CID; his chief constable, Colonel Ranulph 'Streaky' Bacon; Norman Scott's most sympathetic landlady, Mrs Friendship; his kindly Jesuit mentor, Father Sweetman. And then there's the handsome young Buckingham Palace footman who had an affair with Thorpe and wrote about it many years later in his memoir, Adventures of a Gentleman's Gentleman. His name? Guy Hunting.

One dog barks because it sees something; a hundred dogs bark because they heard the first dog bark.

Chinese proverb

Most people are better than you think - you just have to give them the opportunity.

Camus

At the moment, everyone's view is 'hey, why are you so bearish? You know Mark Carney is in charge, he can magic anything.' But why was the Wizard of Oz written in the 1930s?

Crispin Odey

Thirty two religions - and just one dish.

Talleyrand on America

There are two types of people in the world; those who believe that there are two types of people - and those that don't.

Italian has eleven words for a coat hanger - and none for a hangover.

John Hooper: The Italians

Poor Mexico; so far from God and so close to the United States.

Profirio Diaz President of Mexico 1878 - 1911

And the days are not full enough
And the nights are not full enough
And life slips by like a field mouse
Not shaking the grass

Ezra Pound

I remember the first time I had sex. I kept the receipt.

Groucho Marx

Edinburgh pays cruelly for her high seat in one of the vilest climates under heaven. She is liable to be beaten upon by all the winds that blow, to be drenched with rain, to be buried in cold sea fogs out of the east, and powdered with the snow as it comes flying southward from the Highland hills. The weather is raw and boisterous in winter, shifty and ungenial in summer, and a downright meteorological purgatory in the spring. The delicate die early, and I, as a survivor, among bleak winds and plumping rain, have been sometimes tempted to envy them their fate.

Robert Louis Stevenson

The great enemy of truth is very often not the lie, deliberate, contrived and dishonest, but the myth, persistent, persuasive and unrealistic.

John F Kennedy

We are all called at certain moments to comfort people who are enduring some trauma. Many of us don't know how to react in such situations, but others do. In the first place, they just show up. They provide a ministry of presence. Next, they don't compare. The sensitive person understands that each person's ordeal is unique and should not be compared to anyone else's. Next, they do the practical things—making lunch, dusting the room, washing the towels. Finally, they don't try to minimize what is going on. They don't attempt to reassure with false, saccharine sentiments. They don't say that the pain is all for the best. They don't search for silver linings. They practice a passive activism. They don't bustle about trying to solve something that cannot be solved. The sensitive person grants the sufferer the dignity of her own process. She lets the sufferer define the meaning of what is going on. She just sits simply through the nights of pain and darkness, being practical, human, simple, and direct.

David Brooks, The Road to Character

Anyone can achieve the momentary fame; but for nearly everyone today fifteen minutes of anonymity has become an impossible dream.

John Gray

This is Metternich's first assessment of Napoleon - and it is particularly interesting as he later became one of his most implacable enemies.

What at first struck me most was the remarkable perspicuity and grand simplicity of his mind and its processes. Conversation with him always had a charm for me, difficult to define. Seizing the essential point of subjects, stripping them of useless accessories, developing his thought and never ceasing to elaborate it till he had made it perfectly clear and conclusive, always finding the fitting word for the thing, or inventing one where the image of language had not created it, his conversation was ever full of interest. Yet he did not fail to listen to the remarks and objections addressed to him. He accepted them, questioned or opposed them, without losing the tone or overstepping the bounds of a business conversation; and I have never felt the least difficulty in saying to him what I believed to be the truth, even when it was not likely to please him

Everyone is a prisoner of his own experiences. No one can eliminate prejudices - only recognise them.

Ed Murrow

The daughter of Beria, Stalin's sadistic police chief, believed that if her father had been born in America, rather than revolutionary Russia, he would have been the head of General Motors. Adam Smith famously said that a man was most harmlessly occupied in making money. Keynes thought the same......

Dangerous human proclivities can be canalised into comparatively harmless channels by the existence of opportunity for moneymaking and private wealth, which, if they can't be satisfied in this way, may find their outlet in cruelty, the reckless pursuit of personal power and authority, and other forms of self-aggrandisement. It is better that a man tyrannise over his bank balance than over his fellow citizens; and while the former is sometimes denounced as being a means to the latter, sometimes at least it is an alternative.

If you only read one thing this year... Then you're probably the kind of person who'll enjoy this.

A review of Nigel Farage's The Purple Revolution

The greatest thing a human soul ever does in this world is to see something, and tell what it saw in a plain way. Hundreds of people can talk for one who can think, but thousands can think for one who can see.

John Ruskin

It has been said that science can be poetry. Carl Sagan (and Ann Druyan) prove it.

Fireflies out on a warm summer's night, seeing the urgent, flashing, yellow-white phosphorescence below them, go crazy with desire; moths cast to the winds an enchantment potion that draws the opposite sex, wings beating hurriedly, from kilometres away; peacocks display a devastating corona of blue and green and the peahens are all aflutter; competing pollen grains extrude tiny tubes that race each other down the female flower's orifice to the waiting egg below; luminescent squid present rhapsodic light shows, altering the pattern, brightness and colour radiated from their heads, tentacles, and eyeballs; a tapeworm diligently lays a hundred thousand fertilized eggs in a single day; a great whale rumbles through the ocean depths uttering plaintive cries that are understood hundreds of thousands of kilometres away, where another lonely behemoth is attentively listening; bacteria sidle up to one another and merge; cicadas chorus in a collective serenade of love; honeybee couples soar on matrimonial flights from which only one partner returns; male fish spray their spunk over a slimy clutch of eggs laid by God-knows-who; dogs, out cruising, sniff each other's nether parts, seeking erotic stimuli; flowers exude sultry perfumes and decorate their petals with garish ultraviolet advertisements for passing insects, birds, and bats; and men and women sing, dance, dress, adorn, paint, posture, self-mutilate, demand, coerce, dissemble, plead, succumb, and risk their lives.

To say that love makes the world go around is to go too far. The Earth spins because it did so as it was formed and there has been nothing to stop it since. But the nearly maniacal devotion to sex and love by most of the plants, animals, and microbes with which we are familiar is a pervasive and striking aspect of life on Earth. It cries out for explanation. What is all this in aid of? What is the torrent of passion and obsession about? Why will organisms go without sleep, without food, gladly put themselves in mortal danger for sex? ...For more than half the history of life on Earth organisms seem to have done perfectly well without it. What good is sex? ...Through 4 billion years of natural selection, instructions have been honed and fine-tuned. sequences of As, Os, Gs, and Ts, manuals written out in the alphabet of life in competition with other similar manuals published by other firms. The organisms become the means through which the instructions flow and copy themselves, by which new instructions are tried out, on which selection operates.

From Shadows of Forgotten Ancestors: A search for who we are.

Astronomers have discovered a black hole of unimaginable size, 12 billion times more massive than our sun, in the early universe.

The object is at the centre of a young galaxy 12.8 billion light years from earth. It cannot be observed directly – no light escapes from the gravitational pull of a black hole – but reveals itself through the intense radiation emitted by the surrounding dust and other material being sucked into the hole.

The visible outcome is a quasar of extreme luminosity. Indeed SDDS J0100+2802, as it is unmemorably called, is by far the brightest object that astronomers have seen so far in the young universe: 420 trillion times brighter than the sun. That is 420,000,000,000,000 times.

In my next life I want to live my life backwards. You start out dead and get that out of the way. Then you wake up in an old people's home feeling better every day. You get kicked out for being too healthy, go collect your pension, and then when you start work, you get a gold watch and a party on your first day. You work for 40 years until you're young enough to enjoy your retirement. You party, drink alcohol, and are generally promiscuous, then you are ready for high school. You then go to primary school, you become a kid, you play. You have no responsibilities, you become a baby until you are born.

And then you spend your last nine months floating in luxurious spa-like conditions with central heating and room service on tap, larger quarters every day and then Voila! You finish off as an orgasm!

Woody Allen

There's an expiry date on blaming your parents for steering you in the wrong direction; the moment you're old enough to take the wheel, the responsibility lies with you.

JK Rowling

The trees are coming into leaf
Like something almost being said;
The recent buds relax and spread,
Their greenness is a kind of grief.

Is it that they are born again
And we grow old? No, they die too
Their yearly trick of looking new

Is written down in rings of grain.

And yet the unresting castles thresh
In full grown thickness every May
Last year is dead, they seem to say
Begin afresh, afresh, afresh.

Larkin

People who have little experience with power, those who have been
far away from it, tend to regard these things as mysterious and novel.
But I look past the superficial things: the power and the flowers and
the glory and the applause. I see the detention houses, the fickleness
of human relationships. I understand politics on a deeper level.

Xi Jinping, President of China, interviewed in 2001

Into the face of the young man...had crept a look of furtive shame,
the shifty, hangdog look that announces that an Englishman is about
to talk French.

PG Woodhouse

Ask any cook who their favourite dinner guests are and they will
name, not the beautiful and the aesthetic, the trendy and the smart
but those who love to eat. Those who enter the room and sniff
appreciatively, whose pupils dilate at the sight of the viable
deliciousness, who close their eyes and breathe deeply the hot
perfumed air, who use fingers and tongue to tease a bird apart and
lips to suck the juices from the ripe fruit, who do not count calories
or cavil at a little lipsslicking fattiness. Those who are always ready
for a little more. And it is an equal joy to make the two-backed beast
with someone who's favourite animal that is.

Kate Copstick

A thing long expected takes the form of the unexpected when, at last, it comes.

Mark Twain

We can complain because rose bushes have thorns, or we can rejoice because thorn bushes have roses.

Abraham Lincoln

You know you're getting old when you buy a sexy sheer nightgown and don't know anyone who can see through it.

Joan Rivers

No lesson seems to be so deeply inculcated by experience of life as that you should never trust experts. If you believe doctors, nothing is wholesome; if you believe theologians, nothing is innocent; if you believe soldiers, nothing is safe.

Lord Salisbury

H is for Hawk by Helen Macdonald was the worthy winner of the Samuel Johnson Prize and the Costa. It is primarily about a woman training a goshawk – the Mike Tyson of the skies. It is also an account of grief - and a beautifully written natural history and literary biography.

It is bright, after heavy rain, and the crowds of closing time gone. On this second expedition from the house Mabel grips the glove more tightly than ever. She is tense. She looks smaller and feels heavier in this mood, as it fear had a weight to it, as if pewter had been poured into her long and airy bones. The raindrop marks on her tight – feathered front run together into long lines like those around a downturned mouth. She picks fitfully at her food, but mostly she stares, taut with reserve, about her. She follows bicycles with her eyes. She hunches ready to spring when people come too close.

Children alarm her. She is unsure about dogs. Big dogs, that is. Small dogs fascinate her for other reasons.

After ten minutes of haunted apprehension, the goshawk decides that she's not going to be eaten, or beaten to death, by any of these things. She rouses and begins to eat. Cars and buses rattle fumily past, and when the food is gone she stands staring at the strange world around her. So do I. I've been with my hawk so long, just her and me, that I'm seeing my city through her eyes. She watches a woman throwing a ball to her dog on the grass, and I watch too, as baffled by what she's doing as the hawk is. I stare at traffic lights before I remember what they are. Bicycles are spinning mysteries of glittering metal. The buses going past are walls with wheels. What's salient to the hawk in the city is not what is salient to man. The things she sees are uninteresting to her. Irrelevant. Until there's a clatter of wings. We both look up. There's a pigeon, a wood-pigeon, sailing down to roost in a lime tree above us. Time slows. The air thickens and the hawk is transformed. It's as if all her weapons systems were suddenly engaged. Red cross-hairs. She stands on her toes and cranes her neck. This. This flight path. This thing, she thinks. This is fascinating. Some part of the hawk's young brain has just worked something out, and it has everything to do with death.

Leisure, robots and the meaning of money; three views:

There is no country and no people who can look forward to the age of leisure and of abundance without a dread. It is a fearful problem for the ordinary person, with no special talents, to occupy himself, especially if he no longer has roots in the soil or in custom or in the beloved conventions of a traditional society.

Keynes

The ultimate effect of technology, it has been said, will be a factory run by one man and a dog: the man to feed the dog, and the dog to bite the man if he touches the machinery. That sounds fine to me: while patting his dog and watching machine whirr, he could read a book.

Ben Macintyre

23

We have reached that time of year when we traditionally turn from the turmoil of the markets and the troubles with money, to the good life. From the rubble of the rouble, to a sizzling turkey, to re-discover the signal from the noise. But what is the good life?

The journey takes us back in time and to the ends of the earth, to St Helena, where we find a famous prisoner, Napoleon Bonaparte, who is in the midst of a furious fight over the size of his rose garden. Believing himself to be absolute ruler of all that he surveys, he naturally wants to make his garden larger, but the Governor of St Helena is absolutely opposed to this land grab. He had seen its consequences. Napoleon, Ex-Emperor of France and Ruler of Europe, who had commanded vast armies now couldn't even enlarge his own garden parterre a centimetre. His personality blindspot meant that he had lost the plot. His insatiable desire for "more and more" resulted in "less and less". He went from ruler to loser because he didn't know when "enough was enough".
So how much is enough? Economists cannot provide the answer. In society, insatiable appetites are considered pathological, and yet economists treat this mental illness as the norm. To economists we are all psychopaths mindlessly pursuing money, with seemingly insatiable consumption. Don't believe me - if your kitchen ceiling lights look even vaguely like those of Heathrow airport's landing lights, then you will need to think again.

Keynes himself was aware of these limitations and had expected economists to become as useful as dentists, their marginal utility putting them at the very margins of life. Yet strangely, their inability to say anything useful seems to have increased their importance. Believing that money is the measure of one's worth, makes no more sense than to believe that GDP is the measure of one's economy. Why still use a value that is increased by prostitution and yet decreased by voluntary work, like childcare? That fails to subtract the cost of pollution and ascribes no value to leisure? It is like measuring Christmas only by its tinsel and trinkets, which is of course exactly what they do.

Keynes believed by 2030, we would 4x richer, and given the marginal return on income, work for only a quarter of the time. As productivity increased, working hours would decrease. He expected us to work only 15 hours rather than the 50 or 60 hours per week we actually work. He mistakenly believed that once we had satisfied our material needs, then we would enjoy our leisure, spending less time at work and more time enjoying ourselves. But the reverse is true - the richer you are, the more likely you are to work even longer hours. Money has become the competitive yardstick, the way of keeping score. To the Swedish Economist, Staffan Linder - leisure is both a benefit and a cost, the cost of not working. This cost grows as productivity grows - thus the cost of lying in the grass for an executive is higher than that of a student. Weirdly, lower paid workers are working less than they want to and the richer ones are working more than they need to. The workaholic rich have replaced the idle rich or those fabled aristocrats.

Keynes believed 4-8x the average income was enough for the professional classes to live the good life and the equivalent of Euro 46,000 per annum was enough to satisfy average needs. Sums echoed by Balzac and Austen. Russian oligarch's might think this sum is derisory. Putin himself said he works like a galley slave - but he certainly doesn't live like one. He is rumoured to have 20 residences, including the Constantine Palace, a Czarist-era estate, a ski lodge in the Caucasus Mountains and a Gothic revival palace in the Moscow region. He has 15 helicopters, 4 yachts and 43 aircraft. Surely in aircraft at least, he has reached a marginal return, given you can only fly in one at a time. This desire for more and more looks distinctly Napoleonic - especially given his description of 'Eastern Ukraine, with the Czarist term "New Russia." It is not as if Russia is short of land.

There is an old saying: as soon as a man get rich he goes bad and as soon as a woman goes bad, she becomes rich. Echoed by Mandeville's view: "you can have riches and vice, poverty and virtue - but you can't have riches and virtue." Money, according to Robert and Edward Skidelsky, should only be the background noise. A means to help you achieve the good life. The good life is defined by seven basic goods: health, security, respect, personality, harmony with nature, friendship and leisure. The good life balances these needs. This is the signal among the noise. According to Cicero - "if you have a garden and a library you have all you need."

Andrew Nason

In 1934 Robert Pirosh, who went on to win an Academy Award, left his job as copywriter in New York to try and become scriptwriter in Hollywood. He wrote this letter to any contact he could muster in Tinseltown.

Dear Sir:

I like words. I like fat buttery words, such as ooze, turpitude, glutinous, toady. I like solemn, angular, creaky words, such as straitlaced, cantankerous, pecunious, valedictory. I like spurious, black-is-white words, such as mortician, liquidate, tonsorial, demi-monde. I like suave "V" words, such as Svengali, svelte, bravura, verve. I like crunchy, brittle, crackly words, such as splinter, grapple, jostle, crusty. I like sullen, crabbed, scowling words, such as skulk, glower, scabby, churl. I like Oh-Heavens, my-gracious, land's-sake words, such as tricksy, tucker, genteel, horrid. I like elegant, flowery words, such as estivate, peregrinate, elysium, halcyon. I like wormy, squirmy, mealy words, such as crawl, blubber, squeal, drip. I like sniggly, chuckling words, such as cowlick, gurgle, bubble and burp.

I like the word screenwriter better than copywriter, so I decided to quit my job in a New York advertising agency and try my luck in Hollywood, but before taking the plunge I went to Europe for a year of study, contemplation and horsing around.

I have just returned and I still like words.

May I have a few with you?

No one has ever worn more brilliantly the mask of anarchy to conceal the true face of tradition.

Vernon Watkins on Dylan Thomas

The trouble is, you think you have time.

Buddha

Europe was created by history. America was created by philosophy.

Margaret Thatcher

Perhaps if more people were aware of the first wave and second wave extinctions, they'd be less nonchalant about the third wave they are part of. If we knew how many species we've already eradicated, we might be more motivated to protect those that still survive. This is especially relevant to the large animals of the oceans. Unlike their terrestrial counterparts, the large sea animals suffered relatively little from the cognitive and agricultural revolutions. But many of them are on the brink of extinction now as a result of industrial pollution and human overuse of oceanic resources. If things continue at the present pace, it is likely that whales, sharks, tuna and dolphins will follow the diprotodons, ground sloths and mammoths to oblivion. Among all the world's large creatures, the only survivors of the human flood will be humans themselves, and the final animals those that serve as galley slaves in the Noah's Ark.

Yuval Noah Harari: Sapiens

Nothing tastes as good as skinny feels.

Kate Moss

Quis custodiet ipsos custodes? Who guards the guards?

Juvenal

Henry James would be vastly improved as a novelist by few whiffs of the Chicago stockyard.

HL Mencken

Captain James Cook learnt his trade on a Whitby collier running coal from Newcastle to London. Both his ships, the Endeavour and Resolution were built as colliers in Whitby by his friend John Walker. This letter of 1775, to Walker, was after his second voyage. On his third and fatal voyage he was reputed to have been exhausted and not quite of right mind. This doesn't seem to be borne out by the words here.

Dear Sir,

As I have not now time to draw up an account of such occurrences of the voyage as I wish to communicate to you, I can only thank you for your obliging letter and kind enquiry after me during my absence. I must however tell you that the Resolution was found to answer on all occasions even beyond my expectations and is so little injured by the voyage that she will soon be sent out again, but I shall not command her. My fate drives me from one extreme to another. A few months ago the whole southern hemisphere was hardly big enough for me and now I'm going to be confined within the limits of Greenwich Hospital which are far too small for an active mind like mine. I must however confess it is a fine retreat and a pretty income, but whether I can bring myself to like ease and retirement time will show.

Your most affectionate friend

James Cook

He either fears his fate too much,
Or his deserts are small,
Who does not put it to the touch,
To win or lose it all.

The Marquess of Montrose on the eve of his execution in 1650.

When two things travel together, it is tempting to assume that one causes the other. Married people, for instance, are demonstrably happier than single people; does this mean that marriage causes happiness? Not necessarily. The data suggest that happy people are more likely to get married in the first place. As one researcher memorably put it, "if you're grumpy, who the hell wants to marry you?"

Levitt & Dubner: Think like a Freak

It is not what we have, but what we enjoy, that constitutes our abundance.

Epicurus

As we grow old...the beauty steals inward.

Ralph Waldo Emerson

There is no lonelier man in death, except the suicide, than a man who has lived many years with a good wife and then outlived her. If two people love each other there can be no happy end to it.
Ernest Hemingway

Those who can make you believe absurdities can make you commit atrocities.

Voltaire

Pablo Casals, aged eighty, decided to get married to a twenty-year old. In reply to someone who questioned the wisdom of such an age discrepancy....

If she dies, she dies.

We recently sailed to the Black Sea, via Istanbul and the Bosporus. I wrote this blog about that nexus of civilizations.

The modern Istanbul is vast – the sixth largest city in the world – and the outline becomes distinct on the horizon six hours before you finally round the point of the old city with the Topkapi Palace framed by the Blue Mosque and Haghia Sophia – surely one of the world's great views. A sense of history would need to be cauterized for you not to gaze in wonder; and wonder also at the inhabitants of the ancient city of Chalcedon on the Asian shore who were known as 'the blind ones' for not seeing the site of Byzantium as a perfect place for a city. The stretch across the mouth of the Golden Horn up to the Bosporus Bridge is testing on the nerves of the helmsman. I counted at one moment twenty-three ferries – not to mention five small fishing boats and three leviathan oil tankers all crisscrossing the waters opposite the Golden Horn. They are all pros – and I'm not.

The Bosporus itself is, in geological terms, a modern waterway. In early settled history – from about 10,000 BC to about 6500 BC the Black Sea was cut off from a Mediterranean whose sea level was lower than now as a result of the last ice age. The Black Sea was a fresh water lake fed, as now, by five great rivers including the Danube, Don and Dnieper, which are the second third and forth largest rivers in Europe, and it was about a hundred metres lower than at present. In contrast the much bigger Mediterranean has only three major rivers draining into it. Somewhere around 6500 BC the rising waters of the Mediterranean, perhaps abetted by an earthquake, spilled over into the Black Sea and the force of water routed a canyon between Europe and Asia creating a cascade probably a hundred times larger than Niagara Falls. For the inhabitants of the lakeshore littoral this was a catastrophe as the lake, now rapidly becoming a sea, encroached on their settlements at an estimated half a mile a day. It was a flood of epic proportions and it is surely no accident that Noah's Arc in legend came to rest on Mount Ararat on the borders between Armenia and Georgia at the Eastern edge of the Black Sea.

All this has been attested by geologists and biologists who have found in core samples evidence of changes in the salinity of the water and the type of marine life: fresh water species could not survive in the new saline environment though the huge existing body of fresh water would have taken some time to have mixed completely – resulting in a few making the transition. Robert Ballard, famous for finding the Titanic, discovered remains of human settlement about three hundred feet below the current sea level off the Turkish Coast. There is argument about the violence of the flood – but the fact of it seems highly likely.

The Black Sea's strangeness doesn't stop there. It is a continental drain for both Europe and the Russian Steppe. The Danube rises in Germany and is the final destination of most of the rivers of Eastern Europe. With the water has come a vast quantity of vegetable material that has changed the chemistry of the Black Sea. The surface layer is saline $H2O$ down to about two hundred metres. Below that – and the abyssal depths go down to two thousand metres – it is $H2S$, Hydrogen Sulphide, a poisonous and lifeless environment. Two possibilities flow from this. Because neither worm nor wood-eating biology can survive in that environment, Ballard found a 5th century Byzantine ship with its rigging intact. There is also a possibility, remote thankfully, that the marine layers could perform an inversion and the Hydrogen Sulphide rise to the top. The poison gas released would kill everything around the sea's edge and the explosion, if it caught fire, would be one of the biggest the world has seen.

Even though, famously, the Black Sea provides Russia with a warm water port, with its reduced salinity and continental climate the Black Sea forms ice. It seems strange to think of Istanbul and icebergs but in the 8th Century AD the famous walls of Byzantium were badly damaged by ice floes. Jason and his Argonauts on their quest for the Golden Fleece in Colchis - modern Georgia - had to pass the Clashing Rocks which threatened to crush their fragile craft. Could these have been icebergs?

The modern journey down the historic waterway of the Bosporus is rather less eventful but still memorable. The traffic for big ships is one way. As you drive from the Istanbul airport along the Sea of Marmora there are scores of ship lying at anchor almost as far as the eye can see, waiting their turn to transit. Once the metaphorical lights change they process their way through in single file and head east – the majority being tankers in ballast on their way to the Caspian Sea pipeline terminals that provide much of Europe's oil. As an aside, the time taken to extract the oil that has lain for millions of years below the Caspian, pipe it to the Black Sea, tanker it to the Adriatic, pipe it to a refinery in Bavaria and put the resulting petrol into a BMW in Munich is twenty-two days. For obvious reasons you give these behemoths a wide berth, favouring the European shore where the current is less fierce. The surface current flows from the Black Sea towards the Sea of Marmara but there is also a strong current at the bottom flowing the other way. In the days before engines, fishermen in the Bosporus – and maybe Jason on his way to Colchis – used to sling a net of stones on a rope over the side and be dragged against the surface current.

The Bosporus is in some ways a sketch of modern Turkey. Old, decaying wooden yalis - though many less of them now - sit alongside the new weekend retreats of wealthy Istambulis. Fishing boats line the quays of harbours that also contain marinas filled with the plastic pleasure craft of the rich. The Second Bosporus Bridge overshadows the fortress built by Mehemet the Conqueror in an astonishing four months as a prelude to the final assault on Constantinople in 1453. The fort was then known as The Throat Cutter as it cut off beleaguered Byzantium from the Black Sea. And finally, as the Bosporus opens out and you feel the swell of the five hundred mile stretch of seawater ahead under the yacht's keel, there is a new bridge under construction that frames the location of the catastrophic cataract of eight millennia ago. In the small fishing town that overlooks the straight, under the flashing of an Ottoman lighthouse, there is also the traditional Turkey: no alcohol for sale and no women amongst the evening gatherings in the town square.

I've never understood why people consider youth a time of freedom and joy. It's probably because they've forgotten their own.

George Bernard Shaw

But then I sigh, and with a piece of scripture, tell them that God bids us do good for evil. And thus I clothe my naked villainy with odd old ends stolen forth of holy writ, and seem I a saint, when most I play the Devil.

Richard III, Act 1 Scene 3

We can be knowledgeable with other men's knowledge, but we can't be wise with other men's wisdom.

Montaigne

People of privilege will always risk their complete destruction rather than surrender any material part of their advantage. Intellectual myopia, often called stupidity, is no doubt a reason. But the privileged also feel that their privileges, however egregious they may seem to others, are a solemn, basic, God-given right. The sensitivity of the poor to injustice is a trivial thing compared with that of the rich.

John Galbraith, The Age of Uncertainty

Peecrastinate v. To lie in bed pretending that you are going sleep when you need to pee.

To succeed in the world, it is much more necessary to possess the penetration to discern who is a fool, than to discover who is a clever man.

Talleyrand

Be still my heart; thou has known worse than this.

Homer

How sharper than a serpent's tooth it is to have a thankless child.

Shakespeare

Concision in style, precision in thought, decision in life.

Victor Hugo

I re-read some De Toqueville recently and was re-astonished about how sharp and relevant his observations of the USA of nearly two hundred years ago are today.

The American Republic will endure until the day Congress discovers that it can bribe the public with the public's money.

The surface of American society is covered with a layer of democratic paint, but from time to time one can see the old aristocratic colours breaking through.

There is hardly a political question in the United States which does not sooner or later turn into a judicial one.

Complete abstinence is easier than perfect moderation.

St Augustine

De Rochefoucauld was the prince of aphorists. He also rationed himself to one laugh a year - though the court of Louis XIV was not exactly a giggle a minute.

Hypocrisy is the homage vice pays to virtue.

There are few virtuous women who are not bored with their trade.

We can forgive those that bore us but not those that find us boring.

People often complain about their memories, never about their minds.

Virtue would go far if vanity did not keep it company.

Many men are contemptuous of riches; few can give them away.

The BBC is run by twerps who all have degrees in Media Studies - which is like having a degree in stationary.

Jonathan Miller

Build your enemy a golden bridge to retreat across.

Confucius

Never drink to feel better. Only drink to feel even better.

The gods had condemned Sisyphus to ceaselessly rolling a rock to the top of a mountain, whence the stone would fall back of its own weight. They had thought with some reason that there is no more dreadful punishment than futile and hopeless labor.

Camus

I solemnly prophesy that this accursed man [Adolf Hitler] will cast our Reich into the abyss and bring our nation to inconceivable misery. Future generations will damn you in your grave for what you have done.

Von Ludendorff, to Reich president Hindenburg, January 1933

There is still—and I say this with a heart full of sorrow—no Iraqi people, but an unimaginable mass of human beings devoid of any patriotic ideas, imbued with religious traditions and absurdities, prone to anarchy and perpetually ready to rise against any government whatsoever.

King Faisal I, 1934

Even a happy life cannot be without a measure of darkness, and the word happy would lose its meaning if it were not balanced by sadness. It is far better to take things as they come along with patience and equanimity.

Carl Jung

A man is already halfway in love with any woman who listens to him.

Brendan Francis

Why do you weep? Did you think I was immortal?

Louis XIV, on his deathbed

A gentleman is someone who can play the bagpipes - but doesn't.

I don't like country music, but I don't mean to denigrate those who do. And for the people who like country music, denigrate means 'put down'.

Bob Newhart

Big whirls have little whirls that feed on their velocity, and little whirls have lesser whirls, and so on to viscosity.

Lewis Fry Richardson; Meteorologist

No one worth possessing can be quite possessed.

Sara Teasdale

Skinny, introverted, obsessed equally with his bowels and his soul, attuned always to the political currents in India but listening as much to his own complicated heart, he was an unlikely political genius.

Margaret Macmillan on Gandhi. The Peacemakers

The Bubonic Plagiarist

Jonathan Miller on David Frost

He rose without trace

Peter Cook on David Frost

All the world is a birthday cake, so take a piece - but not too much.

George Harrison

All writing is writers' block; it's all so hard. But not tragically hard

Alan Bennett

If people aren't paying you for what you do, they don't value you. It is a really strange thing that you have to charge really high prices or people don't listen to what you have to say. You could be giving the exact same advice, but the more you charge, the more people are going to follow your advice.

Steven Levitt Author of Freakonomics

Like it or not, we're part of Gaia, and like citizens of a great nation we draw power from our membership. In common with all animals we have breathed in oxygen from plants and used it to recycle, as carbon dioxide, the food that the plants provided. Now, through our intelligence, we've allowed our planet to become aware of its environment in space and not only to see its place in the cosmos, but also to grow aware of potential threats, such as that posed by an incoming planetesimal, one of the kind believed to have ended the reign of the dinosaurs. Because we are alive, in a rudimentary way the system has, through us, become sentient. Before this, life existed without knowing what it was, how old it was, or anything about its future. We are now travelling along a path that could lead us to become the citizens of a live, intelligent planet, which might in turn become a citizen of the galaxy. With such a future ahead of us how could we possibly be gloomy, or believe, as today's puritans keep telling us, that we are guilty of some great harm? We merely have to stop making mistakes, or better – because mistakes are inevitable – learn from them and keep our eyes on the path ahead.

James Lovelock from A Rough Ride to the Future

If someone is gay and he searches for the Lord and has goodwill, who am I to judge?

Pope Francis

Never eat more than you can lift.

Miss Piggy

Laws are spider webs through which the big flies pass and the little ones get caught.

Balzac

Love does not consist in gazing at each other, but in looking outward together in the same direction.

Antoine de Saint-Exupery

It's good to die in your own bed; better still to die in your boots.

George Orwell

You cannot always tell what keeps you confined, what immures you, what seems to bury you, and yet you can feel those elusive bars, railings, walls. Is all this illusion, imagination? I don't think so. And then one asks: My God! will it be for long, will it be for ever, will it be for eternity? Do you know what makes the prison disappear? Every deep, genuine affection. Being friends, being brothers, loving, that is what opens the prison, with supreme power, by some magic force. Without these one stays dead. But whenever affection is revived, there life revives.

From a letter by Vincent van Gogh to his brother Theo dated July 1880

He had a genius for backing into the limelight.

Lowell Thomas on Lawrence of Arabia

When you're wondering whether she's his daughter or his girlfriend, she's his girlfriend.

Pamela Druckerman

The answer to the question of what sustained Churchill and the British in the darkest days is that it was his own words. From them the people took hope and Churchill drew inspiration. Bad at many things, Churchill had early made himself a master of language, and it was through that mastery that his career and self-esteem had been nurtured. By the practice of speaking and writing, particularly the writing of a heroicized history of his own nation, he had built up a great reserve of imagery upon which he now drew to forge what would indeed prove to be tools of battle.

Churchill's words did not only touch his people's hearts and move the emotions of their future American allies; they also set the moral climate of the war. Hitler, a mob orator, spoke little after 1939. When he did so, it was to utter threats and insults, glorifying aggression, deriding his enemies. Churchill, by contrast, avoided threats, condemned few...instead he appealed to a commonality and nobility of sentiment that took liberty as its ideal and humanity as its spirit.

He always spoke, moreover, as if the ideal of liberty, though particularly incarnate in war-time Britain, was shared by all who did not actively oppose it, in this way reaching out to embrace as allies, actual or potential, all those not on Hitler's side...Churchill's message triumphed. It was perhaps the greatest of all his achievements. In 1940 his words captured the hearts of his people. And in 1941, and in the years that followed, his words drowned out the drumbeat of totalitarianism that had dominated the airwaves of the dictator years, revived belief in democracy among the downtrodden, inspired a new patriotism in the defeated, created a new confidence, and transmitted a promise of victory that was believed. Morally, Churchill set the agenda of the Second World War. Its realization determined, after 1945, the future of the world.

John Keegan

We learn geology the morning after the earthquake.

Ralph Waldo Emerson, "Consideration by the Way," The Conduct of Life

Every parent is at some time the father of the unreturned prodigal, with nothing to do but keep his house open to hope.

John Anthony Ciardi

Never ruin an apology with an excuse.

Benjamin Franklin

A cynic is not merely one who reads bitter lessons from the past; he is one who is prematurely disappointed in the future.

Sydney J. Harris, On the Contrary

Love is a beautiful liar

The Paris Wife, Paula McLain

Fear is the parent of cruelty.

James Anthony Froude

Greatness of name in the father oft-times helps not forth, but overwhelms the son; they stand too near one another. The shadow kills the growth: so much, that we see the grandchild come more and oftener to be heir of the first.

Ben Johnson

It is a profitable thing, if one is wise, to seem foolish.

Aeschylus

Implacable vengeance rising from a frozen pity. His sympathies cold and wide as the Arctic Ocean; his hatreds tight as the hangman's noose. His purpose to save the world; his method to blow it up.

Churchill on Lenin

I have never been disabled in my dreams.

Christopher Reeve

The only way to tell the truth is to speak with kindness. Only the words of a loving man can be heard.

Henry David Thoreau

Two nations, between whom there is no intercourse and no sympathy; who are as ignorant of each other's habits, thoughts, and feelings as if they were dwellers in different zones, or inhabitants of different planets; who are formed by a different breeding, are fed by a different food, are ordered by different manners, and are not governed by the same laws ... the rich and the poor.

Disraeli. Sybil

The reputation of a thousand years may be determined by the conduct of one hour.

Japanese proverb

In January 2008, there were 12 triple A-rated companies in the world. At the same time, there were 64,000 structured finance instruments, such as collateralised debt obligations, rated triple A.

Plumber's Sex - you stay in all day and no one comes.

A wise man changes his mind. A fool never does.

Voltaire

The optimists ended up in the gas chambers, the pessimists have pools in Beverly Hills.

Billy Wilder

Today, of Americans officially designated as 'poor,' 99 per cent have electricity, running water, flush toilets, and a refrigerator; 95 per cent have a television, 88 per cent a telephone, 71 per cent a car and 70 percent air conditioning. Cornelius Vanderbilt had none of these.

Matt Ridley. The Rational Optimist

Keith Richards: A turtle that's lost its shell.

Losing his middle finger in a childhood accident rendered Rahm practically mute.

Barack Obama on his famously belligerent former chief of staff and now Mayor of Chicargo, Rahm Emmanuel

Maybe all one can do is hope to end up with the right regrets.

Arthur Miller

Plain women know more about men than beautiful women do.

Katharine Hepburn

Supporters of the European project have always held the view that a transnational political union of a democratic kind, which poses problems that are extremely difficult, will be resolved through crises. I heard a private talk by Joschka Fischer back in the early Nineties, that's to say twenty years ago, in which he said there'll be huge crises, it's absolutely inevitable, but each crisis will bring us closer to the goal. It's a kind of classical position. Gorbachev actually held similar views at one time about the Soviet Union. I think myself that the project of creating democracy at a supra national level in Europe, even perhaps with a slightly smaller number of countries, remains in the realm of impossibility. But you see, if it is a folly, then it's not going to be abandoned because of rational argument. It's not going to be abandoned because we've learned from mistakes. It'll be abandoned only in a crisis larger than the ones we've seen so far. And that may come many years hence.

John N Gray

A bull market is like sex. It feels best just before it ends.

Barton Biggs

A wonderful fact to reflect upon: that every human creature is a profound secret and mystery to every other.

Dickens

Live so that your friends can defend you, but never have to.

Arnold Glasow

Friendship needs no words—it is solitude delivered from the anguish of loneliness.

Dag Hammarskjold

If he be a man indeed, he must always go on, he must always endure. Death is an end to torture, to struggle, to suffering, but it is also an end to warmth, light, the beauty of a running horse, the smell of damp leaves, of gunpowder, the walk of a woman when she knows someone watches.

Louis L'Amour, Galloway

I do not believe that any peacock envies another peacock his tail, because every peacock is persuaded that his own tail is the finest in the world. The consequence of this is that peacocks are peaceable birds.

Bertrand Russell, The Conquest of Happiness

Vanity is a static thing. It puts its faith in what it has, and is easily wounded. Pride is active, and satisfied only with what it can do, hence accustomed not to feel small stings.

Jacques Barzun, The House of Intellect

While there's death, there's hope.

On inheritance

All too many people who think they hit a home-run in life - started at third base.

Whosoever plants a tree
Winks at immortality

Felix Dennis

A married couple should be the guardians of each other's solitude.

Rilke

A definition of eternity: two people and a ham.

When we ask for advice we are usually looking for an accomplice.

Charles Varlet de La Gra

Man is equally incapable of seeing the nothingness from which he emerges and the infinity in which he is engulfed.

Blaise Pascal

It is well, when one is judging a friend, to remember that he is judging you with the same godlike and superior impartiality.

Arnold Bennett

When you don't have money you can't say where it's coming from; when you have money, you don't know where it's going to.

Countess Rostov in War and Peace

The rich think that love makes the world go round; the poor know it's money.

The approval presents me with the opportunity to create a balanced and logically laid-out family home, whilst restoring the architectural heritage of the building and also incorporating modern-day features and facilities.

John Caudwell, the mobile phone entrepreneur on being granted planning permission to add a 10,000 sq ft linking basement to his existing 40,000 sq ft house in Mayfair. A fine sense of irony, clearly.

I am king of the Romans and above grammar

Sigismund of Hungary

Never speak ill of yourself; your friends will always say enough on that subject.

Talleyrand

No great man ever complains of want of opportunity.

Ralph Waldo Emerson

Illness is the doctor to whom we pay most heed; to kindness, to knowledge, we make promises only; pain we obey.

Marcel Proust

Martin Amis being interviewed at a literary festival.

You get ugly when you get old. It's all perfectly simple. In fact I can tell you how it's going to go. Everything seems fine until you're about 40. Then something is definitely beginning to go wrong. And you look in the mirror with your old habit of thinking, "While I accept that everyone grows old and dies, it's a funny thing, but I'm an exception to that rule."

Then it becomes a full-time job trying to convince yourself that it's true. And you can actually feel your youth depart. In your mid-forties when you look in the mirror this idea that you're an exception evaporates.

Then, you think life is going to get thinner and thinner until it dwindles into nothing. But a very strange thing happens to you, a very good thing happens to you, in your early fifties, and I'm assuming – this is what novelists do, they assume their case is typical: a poet can't be typical about anything, but a novelist is an everyman, and an innocent and literary being – but you assume that how you feel is how everyone feels, and it's like discovering another continent on the globe.

What happens is you're suddenly visited by the past, and it's like a huge palace in your mind, and you can go and visit all these different rooms and staircases and chambers. It's particularly the erotic, the amatory past. And if you have children they somehow are very present in this palace of the past. I say to my sons (I don't say it to my daughters), "When you're having an affair, keep notes. Hold it in the fist of your soul. Try and remember everything about it, because this is what you're going to need when you're old. You're going to need these rooms, with a girl in each one.

Nabokov said the big difference between people is those who sleep well, and those who don't. And Nabokov was of course a champion insomniac. He has a lovely line in a late novella which is, "Night is always a giant but this one was especially terrible. Zadie Smith says that people divide into the organised and the disorganised. And she's disorganised. But my father, Kingsley Amis, said that a huge division is between those who have a good time with the opposite sex, and those who don't. And you will know in your early fifties how that balance sheet works.

Just to go a little bit later, because I'm 62 now... Another feeling comes on you when you're 60, which can be expressed by the thought, "This can't turn out well." And that's the bit I'm at at the moment. And really that's the arrival of fear. In my case not fear of death, but fear of getting there. So to go back to your question, yes you do look back with wonder at your youth, and you know all youth is automatically beautiful in a way. It's said that youth is wasted on the young, and that's perhaps true because you don't feel your beauty until it's gone.

It's like being as isolated as a man who failed to get onto the Titanic.

Terry Smith on being out of the Eurozone

Outside of a dog, a book is man's best friend. Inside of a dog it's too dark to read.

Groucho Marx

Reading Edward St Aubyn has been likened to eating chocolate-covered scorpions. Delicious....

With her curling blond hair and her slender limbs and her beautiful clothes, Inez was alluring in an obvious way, and yet it was easy enough to see that her slightly protruding blue eyes were blank screens of self-love on which a small selection of fake emotions was allowed to flicker. She made rather haphazard impersonations of someone who has relationships with others. Based on the gossip of her courtiers, a diet of Hollywood movies and the projection of her own cunning calculations, these guesses might be sentimental or nasty, but were always vulgar and melodramatic. Since she hadn't the least interest in the answer, she was inclined to ask, "How are you?" with great gravity, at least half a dozen times. She was often exhausted by the thought of how generous she was, whereas the exhaustion really stemmed from the strain of not giving away anything at all.

As a guest, Emily Price had three main drawbacks: she was incapable of saying please, incapable of saying thank you, and incapable of saying sorry, all the while creating a surge in the demand for these expressions.

A celebrity these days is somebody you've never heard of... just as j'arrive is what a French waiter says as he hurries away from you in a Paris café.

Above all, he wanted to stop being a child without using the cheap disguise of being a parent.

You start reading a novel with no idea where this thing is going to go; you should finish it feeling that it could have gone no other way.

Penelope Lively

The Washington Post's Mensa Invitational invited readers to take any word from the dictionary, alter it by adding, subtracting, or changing one letter, and supply a new definition.

1. Cashtration (n.): The act of buying a house, which renders the subject financially impotent for an indefinite period of time.

2. Ignoranus : A person who's both stupid and an asshole.

3. Intaxicaton : Euphoria at getting a tax refund, which lasts until you realize it was your money to start with.

4. Reintarnation : Coming back to life as a hillbilly.

5. Bozone (n.): The substance surrounding stupid people that stops bright ideas from penetrating. The bozone layer, unfortunately, shows little sign of breaking down in the near future.

6. Foreploy : Any misrepresentation about yourself for the purpose of getting laid.

7. Giraffiti : Vandalism spray-painted very, very high.

8. Sarchasm : The gulf between the author of sarcastic wit and the person who doesn't get it.

9. Inoculatte : To take coffee intravenously when you are running late.

10. Osteopornosis : A degenerate disease.

11. Karmageddon : It's like, when everybody is sending off all these really bad vibes, right? And then, like, the Earth explodes and it's like, a serious bummer.

12. Decafalon (n.): The gruelling event of getting through the day consuming only things that are good for you!

13. Glibido : All talk and no action.

14. Dopeler Effect: The tendency of stupid ideas to seem smarter when they come at you rapidly.

15. Arachnoleptic Fit (n.): The frantic dance performed just after you've accidentally walked through a spider web.

16. Beelzebug (n.): Satan in the form of a mosquito, that gets into your bedroom at three in the morning and cannot be cast out.

17. Caterpallor (n.): The colour you turn after finding half a worm in the fruit you're eating.

The Washington Post has also published the winning submissions to its yearly contest in which readers are asked to supply alternate meanings for common words.

1. Coffee, n. The person upon whom one coughs.

2. Flabbergasted, adj. Appalled by discovering how much weight one has gained.

3. Abdicate, v. To give up all hope of ever having a flat stomach.

4. Esplanade, v. To attempt an explanation while drunk.

5. Willy-nilly, adj. Impotent.

6. Negligent, adj. Absentmindedly answering the door when wearing only a nightgown.

7. Lymph, v. To walk with a lisp.

8. Frisbeetarianism, n. The belief that, after death, the soul flies up onto the roof and gets stuck there.

9. Balderdash, n. A rapidly receding hairline.

10. Testicle, n. A humorous question on an exam.

I didn't know then, of course, that trial separations are nearly always a great success.

Martin Amis

Chess is the conflict between the pain of thinking and the pain of losing.

Everyone's got a plan - until they get punched in the throat.

Mike Tyson

A bachelor is a guy who never made the same mistake once.

Phylis Diller

Technology is the knack of so arranging the world that we don't have to experience it.

Max Frisch

Lord Kitchener had four dogs called Shot, Bang, Miss and Damn.

Everyone takes the limits of his own vision for the limits of the world.

Schopenhauer

The reasonable man adapts himself to the world; the unreasonable one persists in trying to adapt the world to himself. Therefore all progress depends on the unreasonable man.

George Bernard Shaw

Quinlan Terry's villas are exterior decoration of the age of Cecil Parkinson.

Jonathan Meads

We shall not cease from exploration, and the end of all our exploring will be to arrive where we started and know the place for the first time.

T. S. Eliot, Four Quartets 4, Little Gidding

Experience is a hard teacher. She gives the test first and the lessons afterwards.

Honesty has ruined more marriages than infidelity.

Charles McCabe

It takes a woman twenty years to make a man of her son, and another woman twenty minutes to make a fool of him.

Helen Rowland

You wouldn't worry so much about what others think of you if you realised how seldom they do.

Eleanor Roosevelt

Never go to bed mad. Stay up and fight.

Phyllis Diller

Politicians and diapers must be changed often, and for the same reason.

Mark Twain

A man will fight harder for his interests than for his rights.

Napoleon

Life is 10 percent what you make it, and 90 percent how you take it.

Irving Berlin

I don't work out. I'm Jewish. If God had wanted me to touch the floor he'd have put diamonds there.

Joan Rivers

You don't get to choose how you're going to die. Or when. You can only decide how you're going to live. Now.

Joan Baez

The main dangers in this life are the people who want to change everything...or nothing.

Nancy Astor

Life is the sum of all your choices.

Albert Camus

Too many people die with the music still in them.

Oliver Wendell Holmes

Our worst misfortunes never happen, and most miseries lie in anticipation.

Honoré de Balzac

Always take an emergency leisurely.

Chinese proverb

HERZEN No, not at all! Kolya's life was what it was. Because children grow up, we think a child's purpose is to grow up. But a child's purpose is to be a child. Nature doesn't disdain what lives only for a day. It pours the whole of itself into each moment. We don't value the lily less for not being flint and built to last. Life's bounty is in its flow, later is too late. Where is the song when it's been sung? The dance when it's been danced? It's only we humans who want to own the future, too. We persuade outselves that the universe is modestly employed in unfolding out destination. We note the haphazard chaos of history by the day, by the hour, but we think there is something wrong with this picture. Where is the unity, the meaning, of nature's highest creation? Surely those millions of little streams of accident and willfulness have their correction in the vast underground river which, without a doubt, is carrying us to the place where we're expected! But there is no such place, that's why it's called utopia. The death of a child has no more meaning than the death of armies, of nations. Was the child happy while he lived? that is a proper question. If we can't arrange our own happiness, it's a conceit beyond vulgarity to arrange the happiness of those who come after us...

Tom Stoppard: The Coast of Utopia

An enigma wrapped in a whoopee cushion.

Will Self on Boris Johnson

Do not take the donkey of your desires into the field of your stupidity.

Afghan Proverb

No matter how far you have gone on a wrong road, turn back.

Turkish Proverb

Every great man these days has his disciples, and its always Judas who writes the biography.

Oscar Wilde

It's a very funny thing about life: if you refuse to accept anything but the best you very often get it.

Somerset Maugham

A man is not old until regrets take the place of dreams.

John Barrymore

I never saw a pessimistic general win a battle.

Gen. Dwight D. Eisenhower

Good management consists of showing average people how to do the work of superior people.

John D. Rockefeller

Graveyards are full of indispensable men.

De Gaulle

A professional is a person who can do his best at a time when he doesn't particularly feel like it.

Alistair Cooke

Advice is what we ask for when we already know the answer but wish we didn't.

Erica Jong

Religion is what keeps the poor from murdering the rich.

Napoleon

Love is an abstract noun, something nebulous. And yet love turns out to be the only part of us that is solid, as the world turns upside down and the screen goes black. We can't tell if it will survive us. But we can be sure that it's the last thing to go.

Martin Amis

Genius is an African who dreams up snow.

Vladimir Nabokov

All my best thoughts were stolen by the ancients.

Ralph Waldo Emerson

There is nothing more dreadful than the habit of doubt. Doubt separates people. It is the poison that disintegrates friendships and breaks up pleasant relationships. It is a thorn that irritates and hurts. It is a sword that kills.

Buddha

All this will not be finished in the first one hundred days. Nor will it be finished in the first one thousand days, nor in the life of this Administration, nor even perhaps in our lifetime on this planet. But let us begin.

John F. Kennedy, Inaugural Address, Jan. 20, 1961

Draw your chair up close to the edge of the precipice and I'll tell you a story.

F. Scott Fitzgerald

I have spent all my life under a Communist regime and I will tell you that a society without any objective legal scale is a terrible one indeed. But a society with no other scale but the legal one is not quite worthy of man either.

Alexander I. Solzhenitsyn, Commencement address at Harvard University, 8 June 1978

The growth of the Internet will slow drastically, as the flaw in "Metcalfe's law" – which states that the number of potential connections in a network is proportional to the square of the number of participants – becomes apparent: most people have nothing to say to each other! By 2005 or so, it will become clear that the Internet's impact on the economy has been no greater than the fax machine's.

Paul Krugman, 1998

Solitude is fine - but you need someone to tell that solitude is fine.

Honoré de Balzac

One passes through the world knowing few, if any, of the important things about even the people with whom one has been from time to time in the closest intimacy.

Anthony Powell The Kindly Ones

I was last here fifteen years ago; aged sixty; a kid with a dream.

Leonard Cohen live in London

John Fowles..'is the counterfeit who rings true and against which, like a deceptive tuning fork, all gold is tinny.'

Fredric Raphael

Truth is mighty and will prevail. There is nothing the matter with this, except that it ain't so.

Mark Twain

We have as many personalities as people that know us.

William James

To know oneself is wisdom, but not to know ones neighbours is genius

Minna Antrim

Tunbridge Wells is, of course, the Mecca of Middle England's Fundamentalist Tendency. Its villas are exclusively inhabited by ranting, irked bigots who have failed to understand that irony is the true weapon of the impotent. Instead they employ spleen.

They fulminate against: humans, animals, homosexual marriage, heterosexual cohabitation, long hair, shaven hair, pedestrianisation, cars.

Jonathan Meads

After sitting next to Mr Gladstone, I thought he was the cleverest man in England. But after sitting next to Mr Disraeli, I thought I was the cleverest woman in England.

Queen Victoria

Clive James is dying of leukaemia and estranged from his wife. This poetic coda is unbearably sad.

But are they lessons, all these things I learn
Through being so far gone in my decline,
The wages of experience I earn
Would service well a younger life than mine.
I should have been more kind. It is my fate
To find this out, but find it out too late.
 The mirror holds the ruins of my face
Roughly together, thus reminding me
I should have played it straight in every case,
Not just when forced to. Far too casually
I broke faith when it suited me, and here
I am alone, and now the end is near.
All of my life I put my labour first.
I made my mark, but left no time between
The things achieved, so, at my heedless worst,
With no life, there was nothing I could mean.
But now I have slowed down. I breathe the air
As if there were not much more of it there
And write these poems, which are funeral songs
That have been taught to me by vanished time:
Not only to enumerate my wrongs
But to pay homage to the late sublime
That comes with seeing how the years have brought
A fitting end, if not the one I sought.

Memory is crucial, memory is everything, but to retreat there would be a fatal detachment.

Penelope Lively

When you're done with change, you're done.

Benjamin Franklin

When two people part, it is the one who is not in love that makes the tender speeches.

The truth was that he hated the very rich, especially since he was never going to be one of them. They were all too often only the shrill pea in the whistle of their possessions. Without the editorial influence of the word "afford," their desires rambled on like unstoppable bores, relentless and whimsical at the same time.

Edward St Aubyn

Be my brother or I will kill you.

Chamfort on Fraternité

Tyrants conduct monologues over millions of solitudes

Camus

A third kind of intimacy has been imagined, an intimacy of minds, for people who read and think and observe both others and themselves, and for whom life is an exploration. Instead of constantly asking each other 'Are you still besotted with me?' the question has become, 'Do you still interest me, stimulate me, help me, comfort me, and care for me as I change and grow, and do I still do the same for you?' This intimacy is a partnership in the search for truth, enabling each to see the world twice over, through the other's eyes as well as one's own. Penetrating into each other's mind involves neither submission nor domination: the partners try to listen to each other, while each remains a separate person, conscious that intimacy can be a cause of conflicts, or become too close and stifling, or too defensive. It cannot be a totally safe retreat from the hostile world, and the implication is that two people are unable to satisfy each other's needs in their entirety. But their differences make it possible for them to help each other to explore, together and separately, what they could not attempt on their own.

Theodore Zeldin: An Intimate History of Humanity

You can do what is right for the country or you can do what is right for the people but you can't do both.

Theodore Roosevelt

The Gross National Product does not include the beauty of our poetry or the intelligence of our national debate. It measure neither our wit nor our courage, neither our wisdom nor our learning, neither our compassion nor our devotion. It measures everything, in short, except that which makes life worthwhile.

Robert Kennedy

Do not despair, one of the thieves was spared. Do not presume, one of the thieves was damned.

St Augustine

It is a scene of absences and abstractions. There are no mountains, valleys, rivers, shores; no forests, prairies, tide pools, corn and cotton fields, sun-baked deserts; no hurricanes, no floods, no earthquakes, no fires. The only contrast is between an ice-massed land and an ice-saturated sky. The descending ice that links them — the ultimate source of the dome — has the purity of triple-distilled water. Yet it too, as with everything else, simplifies into its most primordial elements, as snowflakes crumble and fall as an icy dust. There is no centre and no edge. There is no near or far; no east or west; no real here or there. Words, too, shrink and freeze, as language and ideas shrivel into monosyllables: ice, snow, dark, sky, blue, star, cloud, white, wind, moon, light, flake, cold.

The Antarctic plateau

From Hitler Youth to Papa Ratzi.

Sun Headline

There are decades when nothing happens and there are weeks when decades happen.

Lenin

People only accept change when they are faced with necessity, and only recognize necessity when a crisis is upon them.

Jean Monnet

Anyone who thinks sitting in church can make you a Christian must also think that sitting in a garage can make you a car.

Garrison Keillor

The merit of The Spy Who Came in from the Cold, then – or its offence, depending where you stood – was not that it was authentic, but that it was credible. The bad dream turned out to be one that a lot of people in the world were sharing, since it asked the same old question that we are asking ourselves 50 years later: how far can we go in the rightful defence of our western values, without abandoning them along the way? My fictional chief of the British Service – I called him Control – had no doubt of the answer:

"I mean, you can't be less ruthless than the opposition simply because your government's policy is benevolent, can you now?"

Today, the same man, with better teeth and hair and a much smarter suit, can be heard explaining away the catastrophic illegal war in Iraq, or justifying medieval torture techniques as the preferred means of interrogation in the 21st century, or defending the inalienable right of closet psychopaths to bear semi-automatic weapons, and the use of unmanned drones as a risk-free method of assassinating one's perceived enemies and anybody who has the bad luck to be standing near them. Or, as a loyal servant of his corporation, assuring us that smoking is harmless to the health of the third world, and great banks are there to serve the public.

What have I learned over the last 50 years? Come to think of it, not much. Just that the morals of the secret world are very like our own

John le Carre

If the US Government was a family – this is how its budget would look

Income $21.7k
Expenditure $38.2k
New Debt $16.5
Balance on Credit Card $142k
Proposed Cuts $385

An explosion in a pubic hair factory (*about Paul Johnson*)

Harrods food hall yields up its dead (*about the Covent Garden crowd*)

Jonathan Miller

Creativity is knowing how to hide our sources.

Einstein

In human relations, kindness and lies are worth a thousand truths.

Graham Greene

Most of my friends seem either to be dead, extremely deaf, or living in the wrong part of Kent.

John Geilgud

A government that robs Peter to pay Paul - can always depend on the support of Paul.

George Bernard Shaw

Das Einfache is nicht immer das Beste, aber das Beste ist immer einfach.
Simple is not always best, but the best is always simple

Heirich Tessenow Architect

Underwater eyes, an eel's oil of water body....crying to the old shape of a starlit land.

Ted Hughes on otters

And specious stuff that says
No rational being can fear a thing it will not feel, not seeing
That this is what we fear - no sight, no sound,
No touch or taste or smell, nothing to think with,
Nothing to love or link with,
The anaesthetic from which none come round.

Larkin

We, who are as good as you, swear to you, who are no better than us, to accept you as our king and sovereign lord, provided you observe all our liberties and laws - but if not, not.

Oath of allegience sworn by Catalans and Aragonese to the Spanish monarch in Madrid.

He seemed to me a man who masked all his feelings; he had a glittering eye, but a cold gaze. He seemed at once preoccupied, knowledgeable, worldly, remote, detached, vain, sceptical, eccentric, self-sufficient, indestructible, egomaniacal, and hospitable to praise. He was like almost every writer I had known in my life.

Paul Theroux on Paul Bowles

Is it probable that probability brings certainty?

Pascal

Get married in the morning....then if it doesn't work you haven't wasted a whole day.

Hollywood saying

Art is either plagiarism or revolution.

Gauguin

The despair I can handle. It's the hope I can't bear.

John Cleese in Clockwork

Painting - the hand, the eye, the heart; two won't do.

Hockney on a Chinese saying

How do I know what I think until I see what a say?

WH Auden

Ar dheis Dé go raibh a anam uasal (may his noble soul be at the right hand of God).

Celtic prayer

If at once you don't succeed, try and try again. Then quit. No use being a damn fool about it.

WC Fields

Never drink to feel better. Only drink to feel even better.

If you're not paying for something on the internet, you're not the customer, you're the product.

I've often thought that Europe is an allegory for the ages of man. You're born Italian: they're relentlessly infantile and mother obsessed. In childhood you're English: chronically tongue-tied, cliquey and only happy kicking balls, pulling the legs off things, or sending someone to Coventry. Teenagers are French: pretentiously philosophical, embarrassingly vain, ridiculously romantic and insincere. During middle age we become either Swiss or Irish. And finally we regress into being Belgian, with no idea who we are.

AA Gill

All you need to know as to why it went so wrong

1999 – 2009. 53pc real growth in spending vs 17pc growth in GDP

Think about this: when you get to heaven you will meet the man you might have been.

Wazawai wo tenjite fuku to nasu
Bend misfortune and turn it into happiness.

Japanese Proverb

Faith is a capacity of the spirit. It's like talent: you have to be born
with it.

Chekhov

Nothing in life is fun for the whole family

Good advice is something that a man gives when he is too old to set a
bad example.

De Rochefoucauld

Love consists in leaving the loved one space to be themselves while
providing the security within which that self may flourish.

Rilke

The absolutists of contracts are the parents of revolution

Keynes

Open up that Pandora's box and who knows what Trojan Horses
won't jump out of it.

Ernest Bevin

Cocaine is not a drug to plug into the collective subconscious; instead it leaves you marooned on your own tedious island, little caring what anyone else has to contribute. Unlike ecstasy, cannabis or acid, it is not contemplative or mind expanding. It tends to kill humour and camaraderie, and renders the collective mood brittle and anxious. All too often it fosters arrogance, anger and even violence. If the idea of the caring, sharing 1990s turned out to be a mirage, and we ended the current decade more atomised and volatile than ever, the popularity of cocaine speaks volumes, embodying the spirit of our age while also feeding it.

John Harris in the Guardian

Be a lamp, a lifeboat or a ladder

Our ignorance of history causes us to slander our own times.

Flaubert

There is always more misery among the lower classes than there is humanity in the highest

Victor Hugo

Here is a you in which my I is reflected. Here is where all distance is abolished.

Montiagne on love

Sentimentality is the tribute that indifference pays to compassion, it is hardness of heart, or even contempt masquarading as feeling and it is to sympathy what incontinence is to urination.

When the father helps the son they both laugh. When the son helps the father they both cry.

Only the very stupid, very rude or very young never lie.

The definition of a philanthropist is a man whose charity increases directly as the square of the distance.

George Elliot

Money is like a sixth sense - it enables you to enjoy the other five better.

Somerset Maughan

To look this cheap costs a lot of money.

Dolly Parton

My favorite food is seconds

Groucho Marx

Most folks are as happy as they make up their minds to be.

Abraham Lincoln

Abe has it

www.ingramcontent.com/pod-product-compliance
Lightning Source LLC
Chambersburg PA
CBHW070317290526
45791CB00003B/1147